BUG LIFE CYCLES

By Rod Barkman

WASP

KidHaven PUBLISHING

Published in 2027 by
KidHaven Publishing, an Imprint of Greenhaven Publishing, LLC
2544 Clinton St., Buffalo, NY 14224

Written by: Rod Barkman
Edited by: Noah Leatherland
Designed by: Dan Scase

Cataloging-in-Publication Data

Names: Barkman, Rod.
Title: Wasp / Rod Barkman.
Description: Buffalo, NY : KidHaven Publishing, 2027. | Series: Bug life cycles | Includes glossary and index.
Identifiers: ISBN 9781534571129 (pbk.) | ISBN 9781534571136 (library bound) | ISBN 9781534571143 (ebook)
Subjects: LCSH: Wasps--Juvenile literature.
Classification: LCC SB945.W3 B37 2027 | DDC 595.79--dc23

Printed in China

CPSIA compliance information: Batch #QS27KH: For further information contact Greenhaven Publishing LLC at 1-844-317-7404.

Please visit our website, www.greenhavenpublishing.com. For a free color catalog of all our high-quality books, call toll free 1-844-317-7404 or fax 1-844-317-7405.

Find us on

PHOTO CREDITS

All images are courtesy of Shutterstock.com, unless otherwise stated.

Cover – Irin-k, banjongseal324SS.
2–3 – sunakri. 4–5 – NIKS ADS, Rajesh Mishra photography, StockImageFactory.com, fizkes, Rawpixel.com. 6–7 – glebantiy, Bachkova Natalia. 8–9 – Sufian Hanif, Skynavin. 10–11 – porramin saefoo, Tomasz Klejdysz, supersaiyan3. 12–13 – Michael_Hadi, Marek Velechovsky. 14–15 – Marek Velechovsky, Animaflora PicsStock, Marek Mierzejewski. 16–17 – pejunk, finding__nimo. 18–19 – Brody O, Kumbang jawi, Brett Hondow, Wirestock Creators. 20–21 – sunakri, DeRebus. 22–23 – Wanchat M, apiguide, eleonimages, Thomas Hochreutener.

CONTENTS

Words that look like this can be found in the glossary on page 24.

A LOOK AT LIFE CYCLES

BABY

TODDLER

CHILD

Each living thing has a life cycle. This is all the changes a living thing goes through during its life. This includes the start of life, growth, adulthood, reproduction, and death.

Human life cycles begin with a baby. The baby grows into a toddler, then a child. The child grows into a teenager and then an adult. As an adult, a person may have babies of their own before they grow old.

TEENAGER

ADULT

ELDERLY

MEET THE WASP

Wasps are insects. An adult has three main body parts: the head, thorax, and abdomen. They also have antennae, six legs, two pairs of wings, and a retractable stinger.

Some species of wasps live in groups called colonies. These are known as social wasps.

Most types of wasps are solitary wasps. Solitary wasps live by themselves.

Scientists believe there are over 100,000 species of wasps.

EGG

The social wasp starts life as an egg. The queen lays an egg in each cell of the nest she has built. Most wasp eggs are small, white, and oval.

a queen laying her eggs in cells of the nest

The egg hatches after roughly a week for most species of wasps. In some species, the queen can lay over 100 eggs in a day.

LARVA

A larva hatches out of each egg. Wasp larvae are pale and do not have legs. They will stay in the cell their egg was laid in for a while. Here they are cared for and fed insects by the queen and worker wasps.

The larvae spend this time feeding and growing. They shed their skin as they grow. This is called molting. A larva will do this around five times before it is ready for the next part of its life cycle.

PUPA

Once the larva has grown big enough, it spins a silk cap over the top of the cell. This is the beginning of its final change before it is an adult wasp. This is the pupal stage.

While in the pupal stage, the wasp develops the rest of its adult parts. The body separates into the head, the thorax, and the abdomen. The wasp also grows legs, wings, and antennae.

ADULT WASP

When a social wasp becomes an adult, it leaves the cell it was hatched in. Then it takes on a role in the colony. This will be as a worker, a male, or a queen.

Worker wasps feed the larvae and continue to build the nest. Male wasps mate with the queen to fertilize new eggs. New queens leave the nest to start one of their own.

SOLITARY WASPS

Most wasp species are solitary and do not live in colonies. Their life cycles still have the same stages as social wasps. Many solitary wasps build small nests or burrow into plants or soil to lay their eggs.

Solitary wasp eggs hatch into larvae and become pupae the same way as social wasps. Unlike most social wasps, solitary wasps usually leave the nest after they emerge as adults.

Some solitary wasps lay their eggs in or on other animals.

TYPES OF WASPS

hunts tarantulas

paralyzes insects to lay their eggs on

Wasps can be found all over the world, except in Antarctica. Each species of wasp has something that makes it special.

SOUTHERN YELLOWJACKET

is quick to attack when disturbed

CUCKOO WASP

has a shimmering blue-green body

END OF LIFE

As with all living things, a wasp's life will come to an end. Queens may live for over a year. However, workers usually live for just a few weeks or months.

The wasp may die, but if the queen has laid eggs, then the life cycle of the wasp continues. Her eggs may become workers, males, or even queens.

LIFE CYCLE OF A WASP

A wasp goes through many changes during its life cycle. Whether it is a queen or a worker, a wasp makes sure that the colony continues, and with it, the life cycle of the wasp.

The egg hatches into a larva with no legs. The larva molts as it grows. The larva spins a silk cap over its cell and becomes a pupa. After some time, the adult wasp breaks out.

GLOSSARY

antennae long, thin parts of an insect that are used to sense the world

cell a small room or compartment in a space made up of similar small rooms or compartments

fertilize the act of adding what is needed to an egg to make life or change the life within the egg

hatches when a baby animal comes out of its egg

mate to produce young with an animal of the same species

paralyzes causes a body part to stop being able to move, which often comes with a loss of feeling

reproduction making more of the same type of thing

retractable able to be pulled back inside something

social to do with working as part of a group

solitary to do with being alone

species a group of very similar animals or plants that can make babies together

INDEX